COATS **Coats & Clark**

# HOME DECOR
## *for beginners*

**CREATIVE PUBLISHING** international

**MINNETONKA, MINNESOTA**

www.howtobookstore.com

Copyright © 2000
Creative Publishing international, Inc.
5900 Green Oak Drive
Minnetonka, Minnesota 55343
1-800-328-3895
All rights reserved
Printed in U.S.A.
www.howtobookstore.com

*President/CEO:* David D. Murphy
*Vice President/Editorial:* Patricia K. Jacobsen
*Vice President/Retail Sales & Marketing:* Richard M. Miller

*Executive Editor:* Elaine Perry
*Project Manager:* Linnéa Christensen
*Senior Editor:* Linda Neubauer
*Senior Art Director:* Stephanie Michaud
*Art Director:* Mark Jacobson
*Desktop Publishing Specialist:* Laurie Kristensen
*Researcher & Writer:* Carol Olson
*Project Stylists:* Christine Jahns, Joanne Wawra
*Prop Stylist:* Joanne Wawra
*Sewing Staff:* Arlene Dohrman, Sheila Duffy, Teresa Henn
*Technical Photo Stylists:* Jennifer Bailey, Arlene Dohrman, Joanne Wawra
*Studio Services Manager:* Marcia Chambers
*Photo Services Coordinator:* Carol Osterhus
*Director of Photography:* Chuck Nields
*Photographers:* Tate Carlson, Andrea Rugg
*Photography Assistant:* Patrick Gibson
*Director of Production Services:* Kim Gerber
*Production Manager:* Sandy Carlin
*Contributors:* Coats & Clark Inc.; Conso Products Company; Kirsch, a division of Newell Rubbermaid

NURSERY DECOR FOR BEGINNERS created by:
The Editors of Creative Publishing international, Inc.

Printed on American paper by:
  R. R. Donnelley & Sons Co.
10 9 8 7 6 5 4 3 2 1

Creative Publishing international, Inc. offers a variety of how-to books.
For information write:
    Creative Publishing international, Inc.
     Subscriber Books
    5900 Green Oak Drive
    Minnetonka, MN 55343

Library of Congress Cataloging-in-Publication Data

Home decor for beginners / Coats & Clark.
       p. cm. -- (Seams sew easy)
    ISBN 0-86573-343-0
     1. House furnishings. 2. Textile fabrics in interior decoration. 3. Machine sewing. I.
Coats & Clark. II. Series.

TT387 .H667 2000
646.2'1--dc21                                           00-034566

# Coats & Clark

# HOME DECOR
## *for beginners*

# Contents

Introduction . . . . . . . . . . . . . . . . . . . . . . . . . . . . .Page 6

The Sewing Machine  . . . . . . . . . . . . . . . . . . . . .Page 8

Machine Accessories  . . . . . . . . . . . . . . . . . . . . .Page 10

Getting Ready to Sew  . . . . . . . . . . . . . . . . . . . .Page 12

How to Balance Tension . . . . . . . . . . . . . . . . . .Page 16

Sewing a Seam . . . . . . . . . . . . . . . . . . . . . . . . . .Page 18

Sewing Supplies . . . . . . . . . . . . . . . . . . . . . . . . .Page 20

Special Products . . . . . . . . . . . . . . . . . . . . . . . .Page 26

Fabric Information . . . . . . . . . . . . . . . . . . . . . . .Page 30

Cutting Fabrics  . . . . . . . . . . . . . . . . . .Page 34

Matching Patterns  . . . . . . . . . . . . . . .Page 36

Hand Stitches  . . . . . . . . . . . . . . . . . . .Page 38

Round Tablecloth  . . . . . . . . . . . . . . .Page 41

Rectangular Tablecloth  . . . . . . . . . . .Page 49

Flanged Pillow Shams . . . . . . . . . . . . .Page 55

Duvet Cover . . . . . . . . . . . . . . . .Page 63

Decorator Pillow . . . . . . . . . . . . .Page 75

Lined Table Runner . . . . . . . . . .Page 86

Quilted Placemats . . . . . . . . . . . . . . . . . . . . . . . .Page 95

Button-tufted Cushion . . . . . . . . . . . . . . . . . . . . . .Page 105

Roman Shade . . . . . . . . . . . . . . . . . . . . . . . . . . . .Page 115

Glossary . . . . . . . . . . . . . . . . . . . . . . . . . . . . . . . .Page 124

Index . . . . . . . . . . . . . . . . . . . . . . . . . . . . . . . . . .Page 126

# How to *Use This Book*

Welcome to the rewarding world of sewing. The *Seams Sew Easy®* series of books is designed to encourage creativity and instill confidence as you learn to sew. Easy-to-follow instructions with colorful photographs and illustrations help you build your sewing skills while making home decorating items that really appeal to you.

Home decorating items are popular projects for sewing enthusiasts, partly because of the cost savings over buying ready-made. By sewing the items yourself, you also get to enjoy the creative fun of choosing styles, colors, and fabrics that fit your personality and taste to a T. This book will teach you how to sew at least nine different home decor items. In the process, you'll develop sewing skills that will help you tackle many other sewing projects with confidence.

The projects in this book are designed to guide you from your first nervous stitch at your sewing machine to comfortable familiarity. Each project will teach you new skills, listed under WHAT YOU'LL LEARN. Throughout the book you will find tips and explanations to help you understand the "why" behind what you are doing. We also have included lots of variations for the projects, encouraging you to explore the unlimited design and fabric possibilities.

Use the first section of the book to acquaint yourself with your sewing machine and the techniques and supplies that encompass the art of sewing. Your sewing machine owner's manual is a necessity; refer to it first if you have questions or problems specific to your machine.

*Let's Begin*

1. Preshrink your fabric (page 33). Cut one 13" x 19" (33 x 48.5 cm) rectangle of fabric for each placemat front and one 13" x 19" (33 x 48.5 cm) rectangle of fabric for each placemat back, following the cutting guidelines on pages 34 and 35. Remember to align the edges to the **LENGTHWISE** and **CROSS-WISE GRAINLINES**. Also cut one 13" x 19" (33 x 48.5 cm) rectangle of batting for each placemat.

2. **MARK** a point 2½" (6.5 cm) from one side on the placemat front, near the upper edge, with chalk or an air soluble pen. Make additional marks across the top every 2" (5 cm). The last mark should be 2½" (6.5 cm) from the opposite side. Repeat the marks along the lower edge. Draw parallel lines across the placemat front, connecting the marks. These are your **quilting lines**. Mark small dots ½" (1.3 cm) from the edges in each corner, on the wrong side of the placemat back.

3. Place the placemat front, right side up, on top of the batting, aligning the cut edges. Place the placemat back over the front, right sides together and align all four edges. Pin the layers together, along the outer edges, *inserting the pins perpendicular to the edges* (p. 43) in the center of one end, leave a 6" (15 cm) opening unpinned.

machine for a straight stitch of 10 per inch, which equals 2.5 mm. Place ...s under the presser foot, with the ... the bed of the machine. Align the ... the fabric just ahead of the open-... edges of the fabrics aligned to the **...m allowance guide (p. 43)** on the ...ur machine. Remove the pin that ...t before lowering the presser foot.

...or four stitches; then ...come to the dot in the ...hine with the needle ...at the dot.

4. Lift the presser foot and turn the fabric so the next side aligns to the ½" (1.3 cm) seam allowance guide. Lower the presser foot and continue stitching around all four sides, **PIVOTING** in this manner at each corner. Stop stitching at the opposite side of the opening; backstitch three or four stitches.

*continued*

*Quick Reference*

**Quilting lines.** It is easier to mark these lines when the fabric is flat, before adding the batting and lining. Use a marker that can be easily removed; test to be sure. You'll find several markers to choose from in the notions department. Use air-soluble marker only if you are confident you will finish the project in one sewing session.

---

The first step in any home decor project is to read through the directions from beginning to end. Refer to the **Quick Reference** for definitions or elaborations on any words or phrases printed **like this** on the page. If the word or phrase is followed by a page number, its reference can be found on the page indicated. Words printed **LIKE THIS** can be found in the **GLOSSARY** on pages 124 and 125. At the beginning of every project you will find a list telling you WHAT YOU'LL NEED. Read through the information on fabrics before you go shopping, so the fabric store will seem a little more user-friendly when you get there.

Above all, enjoy the process. Give yourself the opportunity to be creative and express yourself through the things you sew.

# The Sewing Machine

The principle parts common to all modern sewing machines are shown in the diagrams at right. The parts may look different on your model, and they may have slightly different locations, so open your owner's manual, also. If you do not have an owner's manual for your machine, you should be able to get one from a sewing machine dealer who sells your brand. Become familiar with the names of the parts and their functions. As you spend more time sewing, these items will become second nature to you.

If you are buying a new machine, consider how much and what kind of sewing you expect to do. Talk to friends who sew and to sales personnel. Ask for demonstrations, and sew on the machine yourself. Experiment with the various features while sewing on a variety of fabrics, including knits, wovens, lightweights, and denim. Think about the optional features of the machine and which ones you want on yours. Many dealers offer free sewing lessons with the purchase of a machine. Take advantage! These lessons will be geared to your particular brand and model of sewing machine.

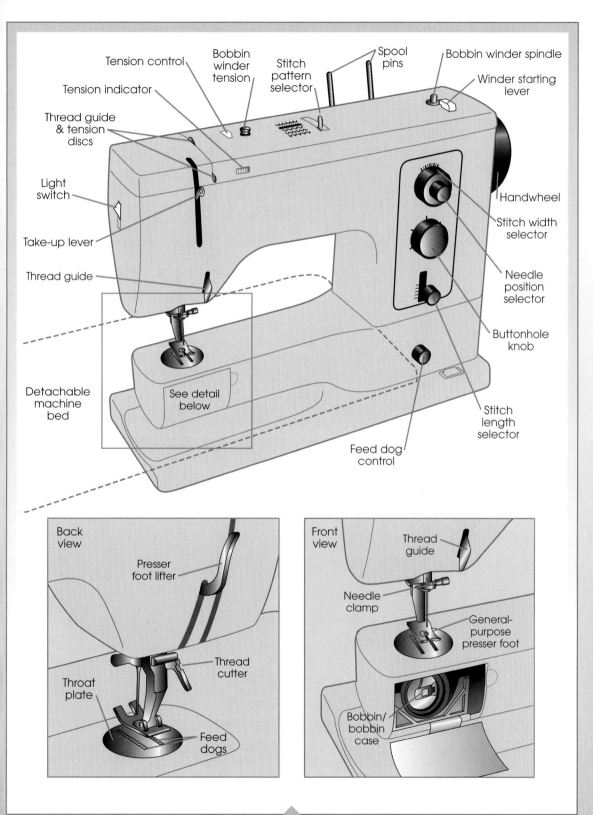

Tension control

Bobbin winder tension

Stitch pattern selector

Spool pins

Bobbin winder spindle

Winder starting lever

Tension indicator

Thread guide & tension discs

Light switch

Take-up lever

Thread guide

Detachable machine bed

See detail below

Handwheel

Stitch width selector

Needle position selector

Buttonhole knob

Stitch length selector

Feed dog control

Back view

Presser foot lifter

Thread cutter

Throat plate

Feed dogs

Front view

Thread guide

Needle clamp

General-purpose presser foot

Bobbin/bobbin case

# Machine *Accessories*

## *Sewing Machine Needles*

Sewing machine needles come in a variety of styles and sizes. The correct needle choice depends mostly on the fabric you have selected. Sharp points **(A),** used for woven fabrics, are designed to pierce the fabric. Ballpoints **(B)** are designed to slip between the loops of knit fabric rather than pierce and possibly damage the fabric. Universal points **(C)** are designed to work on both woven and knitted fabrics. The size of the needle is designated by a number, generally given in both European (60, 70, 80, 90, 100, 110) and American (9, 11, 12, 14, 16, 18) numbering systems. Use size 11/70 or 12/80 needles for any of the mediumweight fabrics you would find suitable for the projects in this book. A larger number means the needle is thicker and that it is appropriate for use with heavier fabrics and heavier threads.

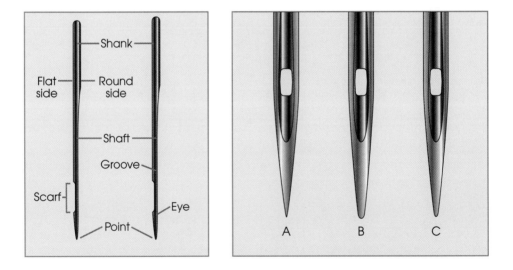

TIP: Though needle style and size are usually indicated in some way on the needle, it is often difficult to see without a magnifying glass, and you most likely will not remember what needle is in the machine. As an easy reminder, when you finish a sewing session, leave a fabric swatch from your current project under the presser foot.

## Bobbins

Stitches are made by locking the upper thread with a lower thread, carried on a bobbin. Always use bobbins in the correct style and size for your machine. Bobbin thread tension is controlled by a spring on the bobbin case, which may be built in **(A)** or removable **(B).**

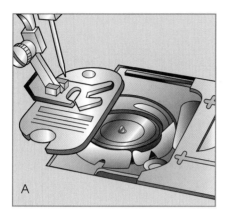

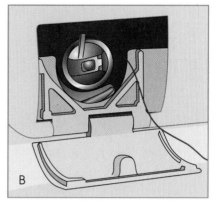

## Presser Feet

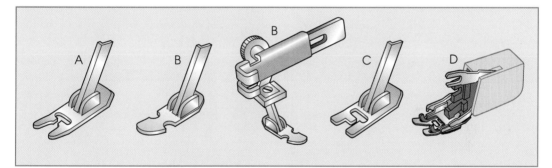

Every sewing machine comes with accessories for specialized tasks. More can be purchased as you develop your interest and skills. Your machine manual or dealer can show you what accessories are available and will explain how to use them to get the best results.

A general-purpose foot **(A),** probably the one you will use most often, has a wide opening to accommodate the side-to-side movement of the needle in all types of utility (nondecorative) stitches. It is also suitable for most straight stitching. A zipper foot **(B)** is used to insert zippers or to stitch any seam that has more bulk on one side than the other. For some sewing machines, the zipper foot is stationary, requiring you to move the needle position to the right or left. For other styles, the position of the zipper foot itself is adjustable. A special-purpose or embroidery foot **(C)** has a grooved bottom that allows the foot to ride smoothly over decorative stitches or raised cords. Some styles are clear plastic, allowing you to see your work more clearly. A walking foot **(D)** feeds top and bottom layers at equal rates, allowing you to more easily match patterns or stitch bulky layers, as in quilted projects.

# Getting Ready to Sew

Simple tasks of inserting the needle, winding the bobbin, and threading the machine have tremendous influence on the stitch quality and performance of your machine. Use this guide as a general reference, but refer to your owner's manual for instructions specific to your machine.

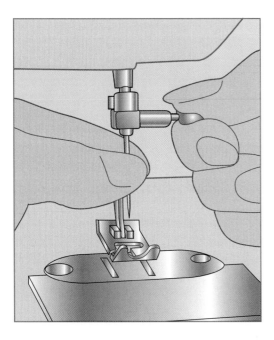 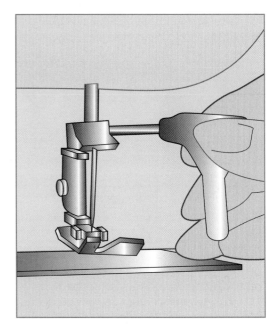

## Inserting the Needle

Loosen the needle clamp. After selecting the appropriate needle for your project (page 10), insert it into the machine as high as it will go. The grooved side of the needle faces forward, if your bobbin gets inserted from the front or top; it faces to the left, if your bobbin gets inserted on the left. Tighten the clamp securely.

# Winding the Bobbin

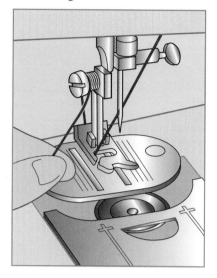

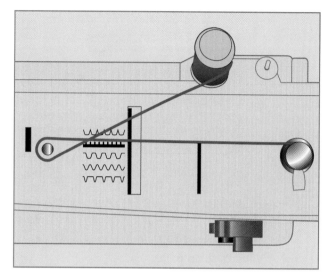

If the bobbin case is built in, the bobbin is wound in place with the machine fully threaded as if to sew (page 14).

Removable bobbins are wound on the top or side of the machine, with the machine threaded for bobbin winding, as described in your owner's manual.

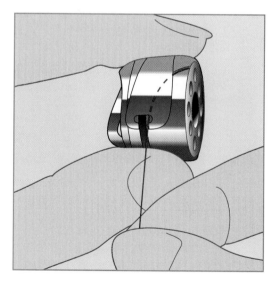

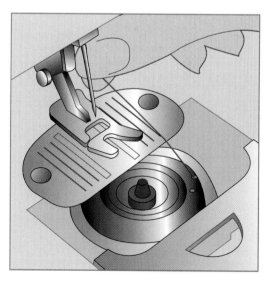

Bobbin thread must be drawn through the bobbin case tension spring. For wind-in-place bobbins, this happens automatically when you wind the bobbin, but you must do it manually when you insert a bobbin that already has thread on it.

*continued*

# Threading the Machine

Because every sewing machine is different, the threading procedure for your machine may differ slightly from the one shown here. Once again, it is important to refer to your owner's manual. Every upper thread guide adds a little tension to the thread as it winds its way to the needle. Missing one of them can make a big difference in the quality of your stitches.

 Set the thread spool on the spindle.

**A. Vertical spindle:** Position the spool so that it will turn clockwise as you sew.

**B. Horizontal spindle:** The spool is held in place with an end cap. If your spool has a small cut in one end for minding the thread, position the spool with that end to the right.

**TIP:** If the spool is new and has paper labels covering the holes, poke them in, completely uncovering the holes, to allow the spool to turn freely.

*Unless your machine has a self-winding bobbin, you will want to wind the bobbin before threading the machine (page 13).*

 Pull thread to the left and through the first thread guide.

 Draw thread through the tension guide.

**TIP:** It is very important to have the presser foot lever up when threading the machine, because the tension discs are then open. If the presser foot is down and the discs are closed, the thread will not slide between the discs, and your stitches will not make you happy.

 Draw thread through the next thread guide.

 Insert thread through the take-up lever.

 Draw the thread through the remaining thread guides.

 Thread the needle. Most needles are threaded from front to back; some, from left to right.

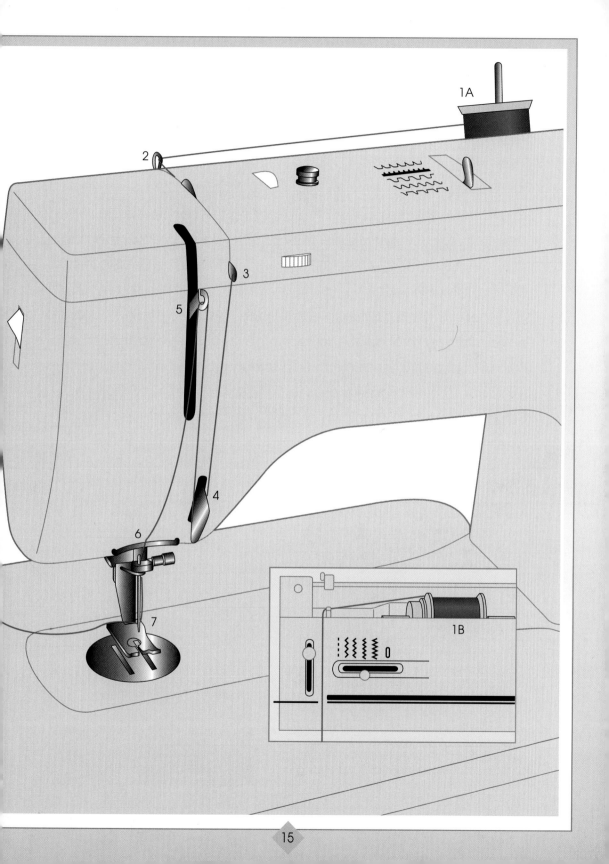

1A

2

3

5

4

6

7

1B

# How to *Balance Tension*

Your machine forms stitches by interlocking the bobbin thread with the needle thread. Every time the needle goes down into the fabric, a sharp hook catches the needle thread and wraps the bobbin thread around it. Imagine this little tug-of-war. If the needle thread tension is "stronger" than the bobbin thread tension, the needle thread pulls the bobbin thread through to the top. If the bobbin thread tension is "stronger," it pulls the needle thread through to the bottom. When the tensions are evenly balanced, the stitch will lock exactly halfway between the top and bottom of the layers being sewn, which is right where you want it.

Some machines have "self-adjusting tension," meaning the machine automatically adjusts its tension with every fabric you sew. For machines that do not have this feature, you may have to adjust the needle thread tension slightly as you sew different fabrics.

## Testing the Tension

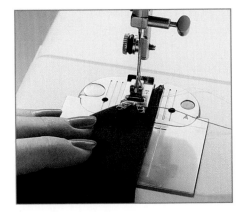

**1** Thread your machine and insert the bobbin, using two very different colors of thread, neither of which matches the fabric. Cut an 8" (20.5 cm) square of a smooth, mediumweight fabric. Fold the fabric in half diagonally, and place it under the presser foot so the fold aligns to your 1/2" (1.3 cm) seam guide. Lower the presser foot and set your stitch length at 10 stitches per inch or 2.5 mm long.

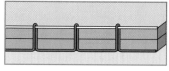 Stitch a line across the fabric, stitching ½" (1.3 cm) from the diagonal fold.
Remove the fabric from the machine. Inspect your stitching line from both sides. If your tension is evenly balanced, you will see only one color on each side. If you see both thread colors on the top side of your sample, the needle tension is tighter than the bobbin tension. If you see both thread colors on the back side of your sample, the bobbin tension is tighter than the needle tension.

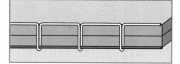

Top tension too tight

Top tension too loose

Tensions even

## Adjusting the Tension

Before adjusting the tension on your machine, first check:
- that your machine is properly threaded (page 14)
- that your bobbin is properly installed
- that your needle is not damaged and is inserted correctly

Pull on your stitching line until you hear threads break. (Because you stitched on the **BIAS**, the fabric will stretch slightly.) If the thread breaks on only one side, your machine's tension is tighter on that side.

After checking these three things, you may need to adjust the tension on your machine. (Check your owner's manual.) Tighten or loosen the needle thread tension *slightly* to bring the needle thread and bobbin thread tensions into balance. Test the stitches after each adjustment, until you achieve balanced tension. If slight adjustments of the needle tension dial do not solve the problem, the bobbin tension may need adjusting. However, most manufacturers do not recommend that you adjust bobbin tension yourself, so unless you have received instructions for your machine, take your machine in for service.

# Sewing a *Seam*

You may or may not be familiar with the very basic technique of running your machine and sewing a seam. Use this exercise as a refresher course whenever you feel you have lost touch with the basics or if your personal technique has become sloppy. Little frustrations, such as thread jams, erratic stitching lines, or having the thread pull out of the needle at the start of a seam, can often be prevented or corrected by following these basic guidelines. If you are really not sure where to begin, then you should probably begin right here!

**1** Thread your machine (page 14) and insert the bobbin (page 13). Holding the needle thread with your left hand, turn the handwheel toward you until the needle has gone down and come back up to its highest point. A stitch will form, and you will feel a tug on the needle thread. Pull on the needle thread to bring the bobbin thread up through the hole in the throat plate. Pull both threads together under the presser foot and off to one side.

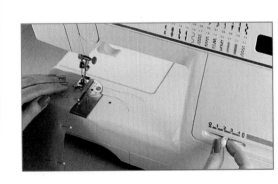

**2** Cut rectangles of mediumweight fabric. Place the pieces right sides together, aligning the outer edges. Pin the pieces together along one long edge, inserting the pins about every 2" (5 cm), perpendicular to the edge. Place the fabric under the presser foot so the pinned side edges align to the 1/2" (1.3 cm) seam guide and the upper edges align to the back of the presser foot. Lower the presser foot, and set your stitch length at 2.5 mm, which equals 10 stitches per inch.

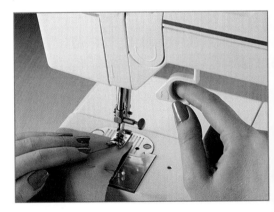

**3** Begin by *backstitching* several stitches to the upper edge of the fabric. Hold the thread tails under a finger for the first few stitches. This prevents the needle thread from being pulled out of the needle and also prevents the thread tails from being drawn down into the bobbin case, where they could potentially cause the dreaded *thread jam*.

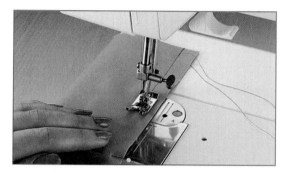

**4** Stitch forward over the backstitched line, and continue sewing the 1/2" (1.3 cm) seam. Gently guide the fabric while you sew by walking your fingers ahead of and slightly to the sides of the presser foot. Remember, you are only guiding; let the machine pull the fabric.

**Backstitching** secures the beginning and end of your stitching line so that the stitches will not pull out. The method for backstitching varies with each sewing machine. You may need to lift and hold your stitch length lever, push in and hold a button, or simply touch an icon. Check your owner's manual.

**Thread jams.** No matter how conscientious you are at trying to prevent them, thread jams just seem to be lurking out there waiting to mess up your day. DON'T USE FORCE! Remove the presser foot, if you can. Snip all the threads you can get at from the top of the throat plate. Open the bobbin case door or throat plate, and snip any threads you can get at. Remove the bobbin, if you can. Gently remove the fabric. Thoroughly clean out the feed dog and bobbin area before reinserting the bobbin and starting over. Then just chalk it up to experience and get over it!

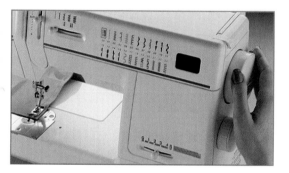

**5** Stop stitching and remove pins as you come to them. When you reach the end of the fabric, stop stitching; backstitch several stitches, and stop again. Turn the handwheel toward you until the needle is in its highest position.

TIP: Straight stitching lines are easier to achieve if you watch the edge of the fabric along the seam guide and ignore the needle. Sew smoothly at a relaxing pace, with minimal starting and stopping, and without bursts of speed. You have better control of the speed if you operate your foot control with your heel resting on the floor.

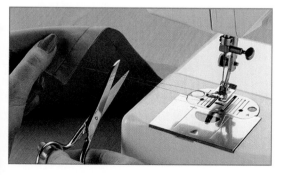

**6** Raise the presser foot. Pull the fabric smoothly away from the presser foot, either to the left side or straight back. If you have to tug the threads, turn your handwheel slightly toward you until they pull easily. Cut the threads, leaving tails 2 1/2" to 3" (6.5 to 7.5 cm) long.

# Sewing
## *Supplies*

In the process of sewing home decor items, you will need various tools and supplies for measuring, marking, cutting, sewing, and pressing. You may already own some of these tools and supplies, but don't feel that you must get them all before you start sewing. You will undoubtedly acquire tools as your sewing skills and interest grow.

## *Pins & Hand-sewing Supplies*

Pins are available in a variety of sizes and styles. Look for rustproof pins and needles made of brass, nickel-plated steel, or stainless steel. Pictured from top to bottom:

Straight pins. Select long sturdy pins with large plastic heads to make them highly visible and easy to remove.

T-pins, used by most professional drapery workrooms, are another good choice.

Sharps are all-purpose, medium-length needles designed for general hand-sewing tasks.

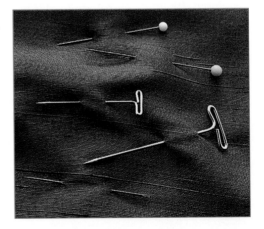

**A** Pincushion provides a safe and handy place to store pins. Some pincushions are magnetic so the pins won't spill. Be sure not to place any magnetic tools near a computerized machine, as the magnet can play havoc with the machine's memory.

**B** Thimble protects your finger while hand sewing. Available in a variety of styles and sizes, it is worn on whichever finger you use to push the needle through the fabric. Most people prefer either the middle or ring finger. Using a thimble is an acquired habit. Some people can't get along without it while others can never get used to it.

**C** Needle threader eases threading of hand and machine needles. These are especially useful if you have difficulty seeing something that small.

**D** Beeswax with holder strengthens thread and prevents tangling while hand sewing.

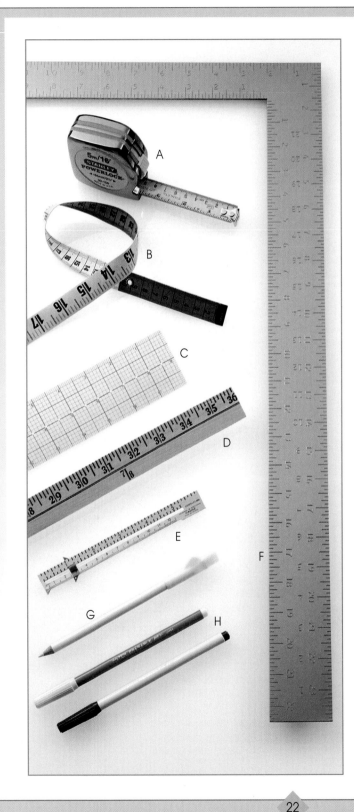

# Measuring & Marking Tools

**A** Steel tape measure is the most accurate way to measure large surfaces like windows, tables, and beds.

**B** Cloth or plastic tape measures may stretch when measuring something large, giving you inaccurate measurements. Because of their flexibility, however, they are indispensable for various other sewing tasks.

**C** Transparent ruler allows you to see what you are measuring.

**D** Yardstick (meterstick) should be made of smooth wood or metal. Use it to measure and mark long straight lines.

**E** Hem gauge helps you measure and mark hems and seam allowances.

**F** Carpenter's square helps you mark fabric for cutting on the straight grain.

**G** Chalk pencils or standard graphite pencils come in handy when marking fabric for cutting.

**H** Fabric marking pens, available in both air-erasable and water-erasable forms, are used to mark various guidelines or points on the fabric. Air-erasable marks disappear in 48 hours; water-erasable marks wash off with water.

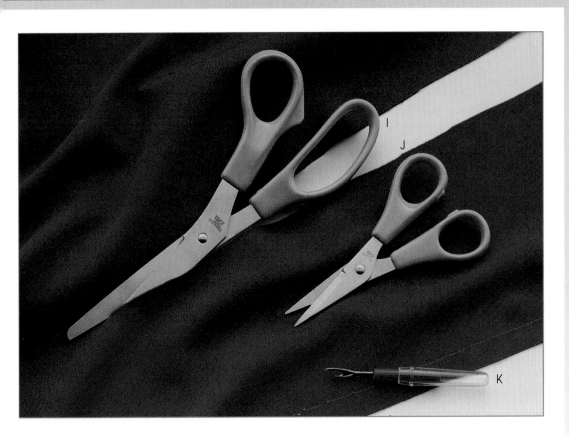

# Cutting Tools

Buy quality cutting tools and use them only for your sewing! Cutting paper or other household materials will dull your cutting tools quickly. Dull tools are not only tiresome to work with, they can also damage fabric. Scissors have both handles the same size; shears have one handle larger than the other. The best quality scissors and shears are hot-forged, high-grade steel, honed to a fine cutting edge. Blades should be joined with an adjustable screw (not a rivet) to ensure even pressure along the length of the blade. Keep your cutting tools at their best with periodic sharpening by a qualified professional.

**I** Bent-handled dressmaker's shears are best for cutting fabrics because the angle of the lower blade allows the fabric to lie flat on the cutting surface. Blade lengths of 7" or 8" (18 or 20.5 cm) are most popular but lengths up to 12" (30.5 cm) are available. Select a blade length appropriate to the size of your hand—shorter lengths for smaller hands. Left-handed models also are available. If you intend to sew a great deal, invest in a pair of all-steel, chrome-plated shears for heavy-duty cutting. Lighter models with stainless steel blades and plastic handles are fine for less-frequent sewing or lightweight fabrics.

**J** Sewing scissors have one pointed and one rounded tip for clipping threads and trimming and clipping seam allowances. The 6" (15 cm) blade is most practical.

**K** Seam ripper quickly removes unwanted stitches. Use it carefully to avoid cutting the fabric.

# Pressing Tools & More

**PRESSING** as you sew is one important procedure that should not be neglected. It may seem like a needless interruption, but pressing at each stage of construction is the secret to a perfectly finished project. The general rule is to press each **SEAM** before crossing it with another.

**A** Steam/spray iron should have a wide temperature range to accommodate all fabrics. Buy a dependable, name-brand iron. An iron that steams and sprays at any setting, not just the higher heat settings, is helpful for fabrics with synthetic fibers.

**B** Teflon-coated sole plate guard, available to fit most irons, eliminates the need for a press cloth.

**C** Press cloth helps prevent iron shine. The transparent variety allows you to see if the fabric is smooth and properly aligned.

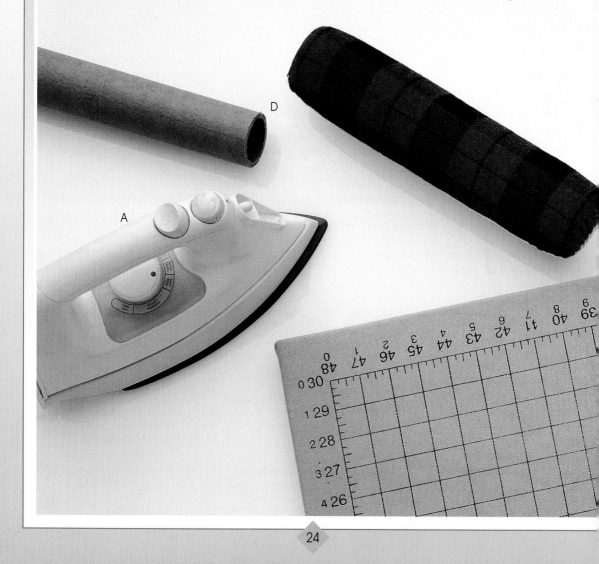

**D** Seam roll is a firmly packed cylindrical cushion for pressing seams. A heavy cardboard tube works well, too. The fabric falls to the sides away from the iron, preventing the **SEAM ALLOWANCES** from making an imprint on the right side of the fabric.

**E** Point turner, made of wood or plastic, safely pokes out stitched corners on items like pillows and placemats. The rounded end allows you to hold seam allowances open for pressing without getting your fingers too close to the iron.

**F** Glues can be used instead of pins to hold trims or decorative motifs in place for stitching. Water-soluble adhesives, such as glue sticks, provide only a temporary bond. Liquid fabric glues can be dotted between layers to join them. Look for glues that dry clear and flexible.

**G** Liquid fray preventer is a colorless plastic liquid that prevents fraying by stiffening the fabric slightly. It is helpful when you have clipped too far into a seam allowance or want to prevent the cut end of a decorative trim from fraying. It may darken some colors, so test before using and apply carefully. The liquid may be removed with rubbing alcohol, but it dries to a permanent finish that withstands laundering and dry cleaning.

**H** Cutting boards protect a table's finish from scratches. Available in padded style, cardboard, or plastic, the board provides a wide flat surface for rolling out the fabric, marking, and cutting. This padded style can also be used for pressing.

# Special *Products*

Many special products and gadgets are designed to assist you in various steps of the sewing process. Before using a new product, read the manufacturer's instructions carefully. Learn what special handling or care is required, and for what fabrics or sewing techniques it is especially suited. Here are some specialized products, available in fabric stores, that you may find helpful in sewing your home decor items.

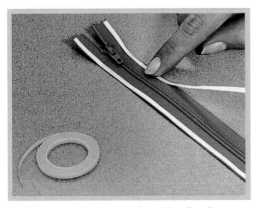

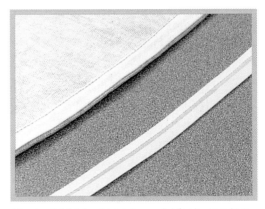

**Basting tape** is double-faced adhesive tape used instead of pinning or basting. It is especially helpful for matching prints, applying zippers, and positioning trims. Some manufacturers advise that you avoid stitching through the tape because the adhesive may collect on your needle.

**Single-fold bias tape** is useful for hemming curved edges, such as a round tablecloth. The manufacturer has already cut the bias strips, sewn them together, and pressed in precise folds to make your sewing easier. The tape is available in packaged lengths in a wide range of colors.

**Paper-backed fusible web** is sold on rolls, in various narrow widths. It is also available as a wide sheet rolled on a bolt for purchase by the yard (meter). It is a timesaving product used for adhering two pieces of fabric together. For instance, you may use narrow strips of it to secure the side hems of a Roman shade instead of stitching them. A protective paper backing is removed from one side after the other side has been fused to the fabric.

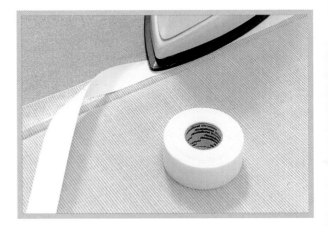

**Welting** is a fabric-covered cording, sewn into a seam or around an outer edge to provide extra strength and a decorative finishing touch. It is available in many colors and various diameters to purchase by the yard (meter) or in precut packaged lengths.

**Twill tape** is a sturdy nondecorative fabric strip that has many sewing uses. For instance, lengths of twill tape are sewn at the corners inside the duvet cover for tying the duvet in place, a convenient feature rarely found in ready-made bedding. Packaged white twill tape is available in a choice of narrow widths.

**Batting.** Low-loft cotton, polyester, or poly/cotton blend batting, sold in packages, is used for quilted projects, such as channel-quilted placemats. It is soft and drapable. Polyester upholstery batting, used for button-tufted cushions, is a firm, crisp batting with high loft, usually sold by the yard (meter) from a large roll.

*continued*

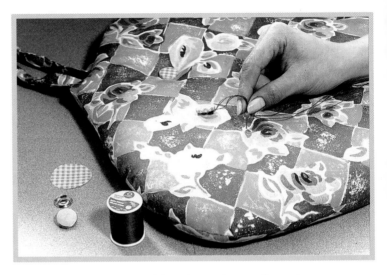

**Buttons for covering** are available in kits, complete with a button front and back and the tools for covering the button. Dampen the fabric to make it easier to handle. As the fabric dries around the button, it may shrink slightly to fit more smoothly. Use the eraser end of a pencil to secure the fabric to the prongs of the button front, working back and forth across the button to tuck all the fabric into the button front.

**Button and carpet thread** is a strong, heavy thread recommended for hand sewing when long-term durability is necessary, such as button-tufting a cushion. The thread has a polyester core wrapped with cotton. A polished glacé finish prevents thread abrasion and tangling.

**Zippers** come in a wide range of styles for many different uses. For the zipper closure on a pillow, choose a conventional polyester coil zipper (not a separating style) in a color to match your fabric.

**Flat decorator trims and grosgrain ribbons** can be machine-sewn to some items, like decorator pillows or Roman shades, for a designer touch. Bulkier trims can be stitched on by hand.

**Pillow forms** offer you the convenience of being able to "stuff" and "unstuff" your pillow quickly and neatly. Inexpensive forms, stuffed with generous amounts of polyester fiberfill, are available in a range of rectangular and round sizes. For extra softness and luxury, you may want to pay the higher price for down-filled pillow forms.

**Polyurethane foam** can be purchased at most fabric stores that have home decorating areas or from specialty foam stores. It is available in various thicknesses, densities, and widths. The store will usually cut foam to the size you need, or you can cut thinner foam yourself using sewing shears, a serrated knife, or an electric knife.

# *Fabric* Information

The creative fun begins with choosing the fabrics for your home decor projects. Aside from knowing you want a certain color or a printed pattern, there are other decisions to make. Do you need a fabric that can be laundered frequently? Are features like wrinkle resistance and stain resistance important? Do you want smooth or textured, stiff or drapable, lightweight or heavy? Some basic fabric knowledge and a thought-out plan will help you make wise choices and avoid costly errors.

*Selvage*

*Lengthwise Grain*

Bias

*Crosswise Grain*

## *Types of Fabrics*

Natural fabrics are made from plant or animal fibers, spun into yarns; cotton, wool, silk, and linen are the most common. Naturals are often considered the easiest fabrics to sew. Synthetic fabrics, made from chemically produced fibers, include nylon, acrylic, acetate, and polyester. Rayon is a manmade fiber derived from a plant source. Each fiber has unique characteristics, desirable for different reasons. Many fabrics are a blend of natural and synthetic fibers, offering you the best qualities of each, such as the breathable comfort of cotton blended with the wrinkle resistance of polyester.

Most fabrics suitable for home decor are woven, having straight lengthwise and crosswise yarns. The pattern in which the yarns are woven gives the fabric its characteristic surface texture and appearance. The firmly woven outer edges of woven fabrics are called **SELVAGES.** As a general rule, the selvages should be trimmed away because they will shrink when they are pressed and cause seams to pucker. Strong, stable lengthwise yarns, running parallel to the selvages, form the **LENGTHWISE GRAIN.** The **CROSSWISE GRAIN** is perpendicular to the lengthwise grain and has a small amount of give. Any diagonal direction, called the **BIAS,** has a fair amount of stretch.

Linen

Silk

Polyester

Cotton

# More About *Fabric*

## *Shopping*

Fabrics in a store are divided into fashion fabrics and decorator fabrics. Decorator fabrics are generally more durable than fashion fabrics; most have stain-resistant finishes. For this reason, it is often recommended that decorator fabrics be dry-cleaned rather than laundered. Manufactured in widths of 48" or 54" (122 or 137 cm), they are designed for pillows, window treatments, and other home decorating projects. One advantage of decorator fabrics is that they often are manufactured in groups of coordinating colors and designs so you can mix and match fabrics for a foolproof scheme. To prevent creases, decorator fabrics are rolled on cardboard tubes.

The designs in patterned decorator fabrics repeat vertically at regular intervals and, when fabric widths are sewn together, flow uninterrupted across the **SEAM,** making seams less noticeable. This is usually not true of patterned fashion fabrics. This **PATTERN REPEAT** is indicated on the **FABRIC IDENTIFICATION LABEL** and is essential for determining the amount of fabric you need.

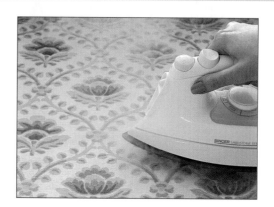

Fashion fabrics are usually folded double and rolled on cardboard bolts. The most common widths are 36", 45", and 60" (91.5, 115, and 152.5 cm). Though fashion fabrics are intended for apparel, many of them are also suitable for various home decor items, especially when you want washable fabrics.

## Fabric Preparation

**PRESHRINK** any dry-clean-only fabrics by steaming. Move the iron evenly along the grainlines, hovering just above the surface of the fabric. Allow the fabric to dry before moving it. Preshrink washable fabrics by washing and drying in the same way you intend to care for the finished item.

# Cutting
## *Fabrics*

Cutting into a new piece of fabric may seem a little scary, considering the investment you have just made. Here are a few guidelines for accurate cutting that should boost your confidence.

After preshrinking, straighten the cut ends of the fabric, using one of the three methods opposite. Then mark the other cutting lines, using the straightened edge as a guide. Before cutting full-width pieces of fabric for large home decor projects, such as tablecloths, duvet covers, or Roman shades, pin-mark the placement of each cut along the **SELVAGE.** Mark out pieces for smaller projects, like decorator pillows or napkins, with chalk. Double-check your measurements and inspect the fabric for flaws. Once you have cut into the fabric, you cannot return it. To ensure that large decor items will hang or lay straight, the fabric lengths must be cut on-grain. This means that the cuts are made along the exact **CROSSWISE GRAIN** of the fabric. Patterned decorator fabrics are cut following the **PATTERN REPEAT** rather than the grainline so they must be *printed on-grain.*

For tightly woven fabrics without a matchable pattern, mark straight cuts on the crosswise grain, using a carpenter's square. Align one edge to a selvage and mark along the perpendicular side.

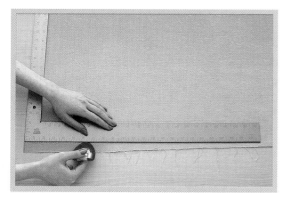

**Printed on-grain.** This means the pattern repeat coincides exactly with the crosswise grain of the fabric. To test fabric before you buy, place it on a flat surface and fold the cut edge back, aligning the selvages on the sides. Crease the fold with your fingers, then unfold the fabric and check to see if the crease runs into the selvage at exactly the same point in the pattern on both sides. Slight differences of less than 2" (5 cm) can usually be corrected by stretching the fabric diagonally. Avoid buying fabric that is printed more that 2" (5 cm) off-grain, as you will not be able to correct it, and the finished project will not hang straight.

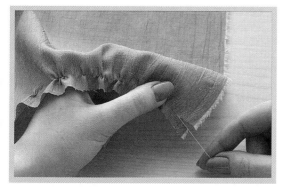

For loosely woven fabrics, such as linen tablecloth fabric, pull out a yarn along the crosswise grain, from selvage to selvage. Cut along the line left by the missing yarn.

For tightly woven patterned decorator fabric, mark both selvages at the exact same point in the pattern repeat. Using a long straightedge, draw a line connecting the two points. If you will be stitching two or more full widths of fabric together, make all the cuts at the same location in the repeat. This usually means that you cut the pieces longer than necessary, stitch them together, and then trim them to the necessary length.

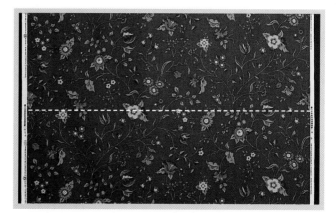

# Matching *Patterns*

Stitching **SEAMS** in printed fabrics and fabrics with woven-in patterns requires a few extra steps to make sure the pattern will flow uninterrupted from one fabric width to the next.

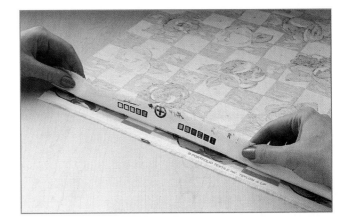

 Place two fabric widths right sides together, aligning the **SELVAGES.** Fold back the upper selvage until the pattern matches. Adjust the top layer slightly up or down so that the pattern lines up exactly. **PRESS** the foldline.

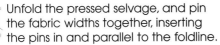 Unfold the pressed selvage, and pin the fabric widths together, inserting the pins in and parallel to the foldline.

Turn the fabric over, and check the match from the right side. Make any necessary adjustments.

**4** Repin the fabric so the pins are perpendicular to the foldline. Stitch the seam following the foldline; remove the pins as you come to them.

**5** Check the match from the right side again. Make any necessary adjustments. Trim away the selvages, cutting the **SEAM ALLOWANCES** to 1/2" (1.3 cm).

**6** Trim the entire fabric panel to the necessary **CUT LENGTH** as determined in the project instructions. (Remember your initial cut length for the patterned fabric included extra length to accommodate the **PATTERN REPEAT**.)

# Hand *Stitches*

While modern sewers rely on sewing machines for speedy construction, there are situations when hand stitching is necessary or preferable. You may need to slipstitch an opening closed in a pillow or lined table runner. Of course, you'll also need to sew on buttons.

## Threading the Needle

Insert the thread end through the needle's eye, for sewing with a single strand. Or fold the thread in half, and insert the fold through the eye, for sewing with a double strand. Pull through about 8" (20.5 cm). Wrap the other end(s)

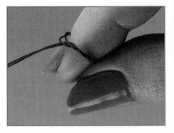

around your index finger. Then, using your thumb, roll the thread off your finger, twisting it into a knot.

TIP: Use a single strand when slipstitching or hemming. Use a double strand when sewing on buttons. To avoid tangles, begin with thread no longer than 18" (46 cm) from the needle to the knot. Run the thread through beeswax (page 21), if desired.

## Slipstitching

 **1** Insert the threaded needle between the **SEAM ALLOWANCE** and the outer fabric, just behind the opening. Bring it to the outside in the seamline. If you are right-handed, work from right to left; lefties work from left to right.

**2** Insert the needle into the fold just behind where the thread came up, and run it inside the fold for about 1/4" (6 mm). Bring the needle out, and draw the thread snug. Take your next stitch in the opposite fold, inserting the needle directly across from the previous stitch.

**3** Continue, crossing from one fold to the other, until you have sewn past the opening. Secure the thread with several tiny stitches in the seamline. Then take a long stitch, and pull it tight. Clip the thread at the surface, and let the tail disappear inside.

# Sewing on a Shank Button

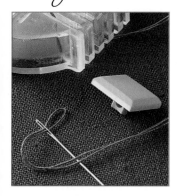

**1** Place the button on the mark, with the shank hole parallel to the buttonhole. Secure the thread on the right side of the fabric with a small stitch under the button.

**2** Bring the needle through the shank hole. Insert the needle down through the fabric and pull the thread through. Take four to six stitches in this manner.

**3** Secure the thread in the fabric under the button by making a knot or by taking several small stitches. Clip the thread ends.

# Sewing on a Sew-through Button

**1** Place the button on the mark, with the holes lining up parallel to the buttonhole. Bring the needle through the fabric from the underside and up through one hole in the button. Insert the needle into another hole and through the fabric layers.

**2** Slip a toothpick, match, or sewing machine needle between the thread and the button to form a shank. Take three or four stitches through each pair of holes. Bring the needle and thread to the right side under the button. Remove the toothpick.

**3** Wind the thread two or three times around the button stitches to form the shank. Secure the thread on the right side under the button, by making a knot or taking several small stitches. Clip the threads close to the knot.

*Let's Begin*

 **1** Cut off the **SELVAGES** from the fabric. Cut out square napkins, following the **GRAINLINES** exactly. Pull threads out of the crosswise and lengthwise grains to mark the cutting lines, if possible (page 35). For the most efficient use of your fabric, divide the full width of 45", 48", or 54" (115, 122, or 137 cm) fabric into three equal squares. If your fabric is 60" (152.5 cm) wide, cut either four 15" (38 cm) or three 20" (51 cm) napkins.

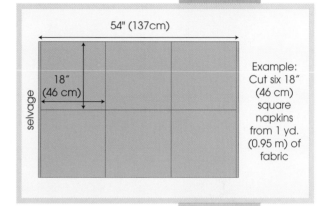

54" (137cm)

selvage

18" (46 cm)

Example: Cut six 18" (46 cm) square napkins from 1 yd. (0.95 m) of fabric

 **2** Set your machine for a narrow **ZIGZAG STITCH,** about 12 stitches per inch, which equals 2 mm. Stitch 1/2" (1.3 cm) from the edge around each napkin, pivoting 1/2" (1.3 cm) from the corners.

 **3** Pull threads to fray the outer edges on each side of the napkin, working from the cut edges up to the stitching.

*What could be easier?*

*And think of the money you've saved!*

# MORE
## *Table Runners & Placemats*

Use a dinner plate to round off the corners of a rectangle creating an oval table runner or placemats. Omit batting in the placemats and add welting to the outer seam. Remember to ease (not stretch) the welting around the curves.

Sew placemats from checked fabric and quilt them, following the lines of the check. Sew matching napkins, following the general directions for a rectangular tablecloth (page 49), but using ¼" (6 mm) double-fold hems.

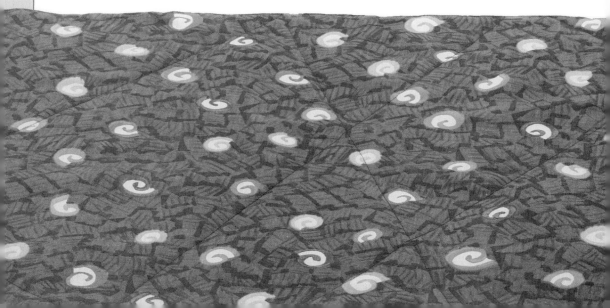

Make octagonal placemats. Prepare a paper pattern; cut off the corners diagonally, 3½" (9 cm) from the corners. Plan your quilting lines to echo the shape of the placemat.

Omit the welting; add batting between the layers of a table runner, and quilt it in random diagonal lines. Sew colorful buttons along the angled ends of the table runner.

# *Button-tufted* Cushion

Button-tufted cushions can be custom shaped to fit chairs, benches, or window seats. They have inner cores of batting-wrapped foam and can be anchored to the furniture with fabric ties. Buttons keep the filling from shifting and accent the "stuffed" appearance of the cushion. Since tufted cushion covers are not usually removed, zippers or other closures are not necessary. Tightly woven decorator fabric with a stain-resistant finish, available in endless colors and designs, is a great choice for this project.

## WHAT YOU'LL LEARN

How to make a simple foam and batting cushion and a cover to fit it

How to make ties

How to button-tuft a cushion

## WHAT YOU'LL NEED

Fabric, amount determined after making pattern

Polyurethane foam (page 29), 1" (2.5 cm) thick

Polyester upholstery batting (page 27)

Thread to match

Buttons to cover (page 28); two for each button tuft

Button and carpet thread (page 28)

Long needle with a large eye

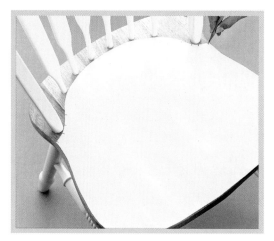

*Let's Begin*

**1** Make a paper pattern of the seat to be covered by the cushion, rounding any sharp corners. Simplify the shape as much as you can. Cut out the pattern and check it for **symmetry** and fit. Mark the pattern where the ties would be placed.

TIP: A piece of wrapping paper or newsprint will make a sturdy pattern. You will be using this pattern for the foam, the batting, and the fabric.

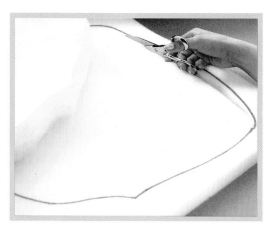

**2** Cut two pieces of polyester upholstery batting, using the pattern for size. Place the pattern on the foam and trace around it, using a felt-tip pen. **Cut the foam** 1/4" (6 mm) inside the marked line.

**3** Place the pattern on the right side of the decorator fabric. **MARK** the cutting line 1" (2.5 cm) from the edge of the pattern; this allows for 1/2" (1.3 cm) **SEAM ALLOWANCES** and 1/2" (1.3 cm) for the thickness of the foam and batting. Cut the cushion top out on the marked line. Cut the cushion bottom, using the top as a pattern. Remember to **cut the covers on straight grain**. Transfer any marks for ties from the pattern to the cushion front. Omit steps 4 to 6 if your cushion will not have ties.

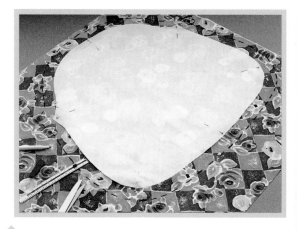

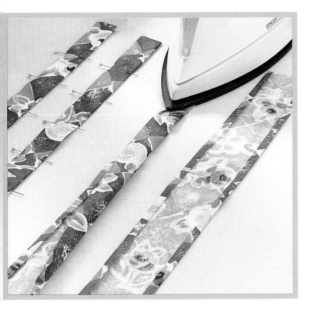

**Symmetry.** Hand-drawn patterns can easily turn out a bit askew. Fold the pattern in half to check that the edges are identical and make any necessary adjustments. Then recheck it on the seat.

**Cut the foam.** Polyurethane foam with a thickness of 1" (2.5 cm) can be easily cut with sewing shears. Other options include a serrated kitchen knife or an electric knife. Be sure to hold the blade perpendicular to the foam as you cut. Some fabric stores will cut the foam for you if you prepare your pattern before you go shopping.

**Cut the covers on straight grain.** Ideally, the center of the cushion, front to back, runs on the **LENGTHWISE GRAIN** of the fabric. If you are using a **DIRECTIONAL PRINT,** cut the pieces so the top of the design is at the back of the cushion. Center large design motifs.

**4** Cut two 2½" × 16" (6.5 × 40.5 cm) fabric strips for each tie, following fabric grainlines. **PRESS** under ¼" (6 mm) on the long edges of each strip. Then press them in half lengthwise, wrong sides together, aligning the pressed edges. Pin.

**5** Set the machine for a straight stitch of 10 stitches per inch, which equals 2.5 mm. **Edgestitch (p. 51)** along the open edge of each tie. Leave both ends of the ties open. Tie a single knot at one end of each tie, enclosing the raw edges in the knot.

*continued*

*continued*

**6** Pin the unfinished ends of the ties to the right side of the cushion front at the marked positions. Stitch the ties in place ³⁄8" (1 cm) from the edge, *removing the pins as you come to them (p. 45).*

**TIP:** To make sure the ties don't get in the way when you stitch the outer seam, pin the free ends to the cushion front. Use safety pins to avoid scratching your hands when you turn the cover right side out.

**8** Place the pieces under the presser foot, just ahead of the opening. Align the cut edges to the ¹⁄2" (1.3 cm) *seam allowance guide (p. 43).* Remove the pin that marks the opening, before lowering the presser foot.

**7** Place the cushion top and bottom right sides together, aligning the outer edges; pin, *inserting the pins perpendicular to the edges (page 43). Leave an opening for insert-ing the foam.*

**Backstitch (p. 19)** three or four stitches; stop. Then, stitching forward, stitch the seam on all sides. End the seam at the opposite side of the opening; backstitch three or four stitches.

**Clip the seam allowances** of any curved areas. Press the seam flat. **Turn back the top seam allowance (p. 79),** and press, using light pressure with the tip of your iron down the crease of the seam. Press back 1/2" (1.3 cm) seam allowance on the cushion cover back in the open area.

**Leave an opening for inserting the foam.** The size of the opening depends on the size of the cushion. For chair seats, leave at least 8" (20.5 cm) at the back of the cushion; for longer cushions, leave an entire short end open.

**Clip the seam allowance.** Before turning a curved seam right side out, clip the seam allowance perpendicular to the stitches every 1/4" to 1/2" (6 mm to 1.3 cm). This allows the seam to open up for pressing or to lie along the edge without any bubbles or folds. Clip up to, but not through, the stitches. The sharper the curve, the closer together the clips should be.

Reach in through the opening to turn the cushion cover completely right side out. Press lightly, centering the seam around the outer edge. Make sure the ties are sewn securely into the seam at the correct positions.

*continued*

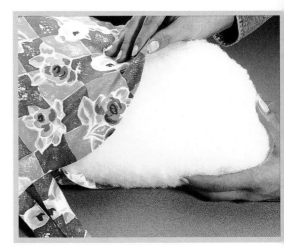

 **12** Place the foam between the layers of upholstery batting. Hand-stitch the edges of the batting together, encasing the foam.

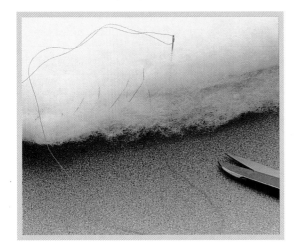

**13** Fold the batted foam in half and insert it into the cushion cover. Unfold the foam, smoothing the fabric over the batting. Slip-stitch (page 38) the opening closed. You can use your cushion like this if you prefer. However, if you want to add button tufting, continue with the next steps.

**14** **Mark the button placement** on both sides of the cushion. Follow the manufacturer's directions for making covered buttons and the general guidelines on page 28. You will need two buttons for every tuft.

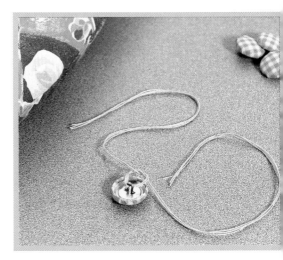

**15** Cut two or three 18" (46 cm) strands of button and carpet thread (page 28); insert all the strands through the button shank, and secure at the middle of the thread with a double knot.

***Mark the button placement.*** Button placements are usually equally spaced in all directions. Use the pattern piece to plan out the placement, trying different arrangements. A chair seat, for instance, can have four buttons arranged in a square or a fifth button in the center.

**16** Insert the ends of the thread strands through the eye of a long needle. Insert the needle through the cushion to the back side. Remove the strands from the needle and divide them into two groups.

**17** Thread a second button onto one group of threads. Tie a single knot, using both thread groups; pull the strands until the buttons are tight against the cushion, creating an indentation. Wrap the thread two or three times around the button shank and tie a double knot. Trim the thread tails so they are hidden under the button, but not so short that the knot could loosen. Repeat steps 15 to 17 for each tuft, keeping the indentations equal.

TIP: A drop of liquid fray preventer (page 25) on the double knots would secure them permanently.

*Give your cushion a proud squeeze!*
*Tie it to your chair or place it on the waiting bench or window seat. Go ahead . . . sit down!*

# GREAT IDEAS
## FOR
### *Cushions*

*Sew welting to the cushion front piece before adding ties or sewing it to the back. Follow pages 89 to 91, steps 4 to 10. (top left)*

*Sew pregathered ruffles or eyelet trim to the cushion front piece before sewing it to the back. Begin and end the trim at the ties, avoiding the cushion back. (top middle)*

*Make a removable cushion cover by eliminating the button tufting and adding a zipper along a straight side of the cushion. Follow the directions for zipper application on pages 80 to 83. (top right)*

*Sew elegant cushions with fancy chair ties instead of fabric ties. These lengths of decorative cording with attached tassels are found in many styles and colors in the decorator department of a fabric store.*

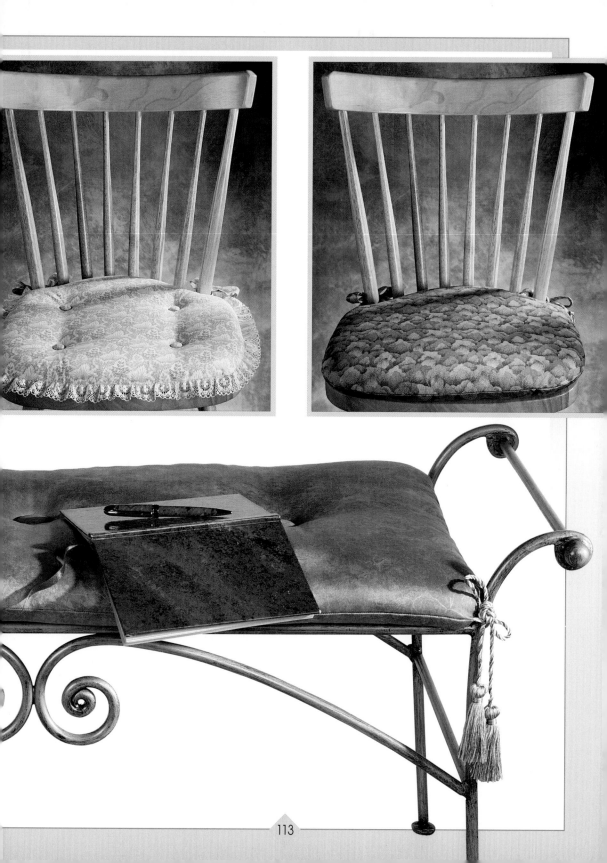

A

B

# *Roman*
# Shade

A Roman shade is a tailored, economical window treatment that controls light and provides privacy. This version is **LINED** to provide added body, prevent fabric fading, and create a uniform appearance from the outside. Mounted on a board, the shade can be installed as an **INSIDE MOUNT (A),** securing it inside the upper window frame, flush with the front of the frame. For an **OUTSIDE MOUNT (B),** the shade is installed on the wall at least 1" (2.5 cm) above the frame. Choose a sturdy, firm decorator fabric to give the shade a crisp look. These directions are suitable for a shade that is at least 2" (5 cm) narrower than the fabric width.

## WHAT YOU'LL LEARN

The importance of accurate measuring and cutting

How to cover and install a mounting board

A simple way to line a window treatment

How to use fusible web

How a Roman shade actually works

## WHAT YOU'LL NEED

Decorator fabric, amount determined in step 4

Drapery lining fabric, amount equal to shade fabric

Thread to match

Mounting board, 1 × 2 **NOMINAL LUMBER**

White glue

1" (2.5 cm) angle irons, for outside mount

3/4" (2 cm) paper-backed fusible web (page 26)

Graph paper

Screw eyes

Plastic rings, 3/8" or 1/2" (1 or 1.3 cm)

Shade cord

Flat metal weight bar, 1/2" (1.3 cm) wide, cut 1/2" (1.3 cm) shorter than finished width of shade

Awning cleat

Staple gun and staples

Drapery pull (optional)

*Let's Begin*

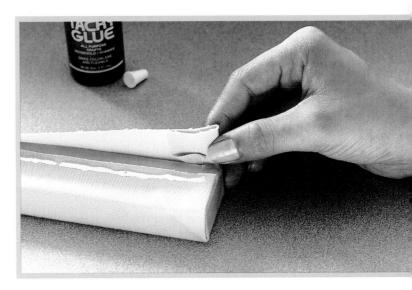

TIP: Nominal lumber, angle irons, screw eyes, flat metal bars, awning cleats, and drapery pulls can all be purchased at a hardware store. If you do not have the proper tools, ask them to cut the lumber and metal bar to the size you need.

**1** Measure the width of the window frame. Cut a 1 × 2 board 2" (5 cm) longer than the outside measurement, for an outside mount or 1/2" (1.3 cm) shorter than the inside measurement, for an inside mount. Cut a strip of fabric for covering the board 1/2" (1.3 cm) wider than the board circumference and 2" (5 cm) longer than the board length. Center the board on the strip; wrap the fabric over the ends, and secure with glue. Then wrap the length of the board overlapping the fabric down the center of one side and folding out excess fabric neatly at the ends; secure with glue. Allow to dry. Disregar steps 2 and 3 if you are installing an inside mount.

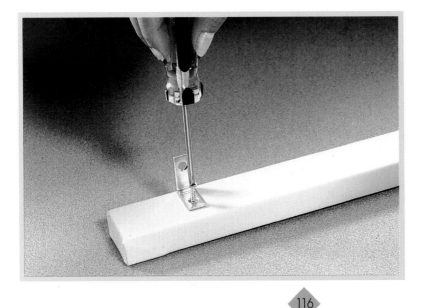

**2** Place the 1" (2.5 cm angle irons on the side of the board opposite the overlap, about 2" (5 cm) from eac end of the board. Mark th screw holes and, using a drill and appropriate drill bit, predrill holes into the board for the screws. Screw the angle irons to the board.

**Plus 1/4" (6 mm)**. By sewing the shade slightly wider than the mounting board, you are sure to cover the entire board. There is always a little width and length lost in pressing and stitching the fabric.

Hold the board above the window, making sure it is level and centered over the window frame; mark the screw holes on the wall. Secure the angle irons to the wall, using 1 1/2" (3.8 cm) flat-head screws. If the angle irons are not at wall studs, use molly bolts or plastic anchors.

Determine the **FIN- ISHED LENGTH** of the shade. For an outside mount, measure from the top of the mounting board to the sill or 1/2" (1.3 cm) below the apron; for an inside mount, measure the inside frame to the sill. The **FINISHED WIDTH** of the shade is equal to the length of the mounting board **plus 1/4" (6 mm)**.

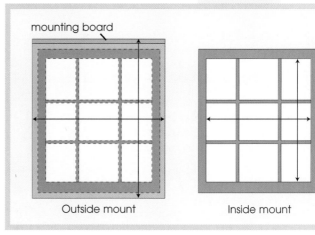

mounting board

Outside mount      Inside mount

*continued*

*continued*

| | | |
|---|---|---|
| Finished width: | 45" | (115 cm) |
| Add 2" ( 5 cm) for side hems + | 2" | (5 cm) |
| to find the cut width = | 47" | (120 cm) |
| | | |
| Finished length: | 50" | (127 cm) |
| Add 7" (18 cm) for hem and mounting + | 7" | (18 cm) |
| to find the cut length = | 57" | (144.5 cm) |

 **5** Calculate the **CUT LENGTH** and **CUT WIDTH** of the fabric, working with this formula. (We used these numbers for our Roman shade on page 114; your numbers will probably be different.) Cut the shade fabric; do not use a **SELVAGE** as an edge. Cut the lining fabric with the width equal to the finished width and the length equal to the finished length plus 3½" (9 cm). Follow the guidelines for cutting decorator fabric on pages 34 and 35.

**6** **PRESS** under 1" (2.5 cm) on the sides of the shade. Cut strips of ¾" (2 cm) paper-backed fusible web the length of each side. Turn back the hem and place the strips near the cut edge. Press over the strips to fuse them to the hem allowance, following the manufacturer's directions.

**TIP:** Use a press cloth (page 24) to prevent any fusible adhesive from messing up the sole plate of your iron.

**7** Place the lining over the shade fabric, wrong sides together, with the lower edge of the lining 3½" (9 cm) above the lower edge of the shade fabric; tuck the lining under the side hems. Remove the protective paper backing from the fusible web, and press to fuse the hems in place.

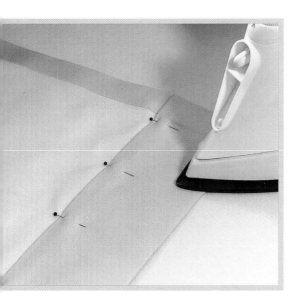

**Mounting board projection.** The actual width of 1 x 2 nominal lumber is 1½" (3.8 cm) which is how far the front of the mounting board (and the shade) will stand away from the wall on an outside mount.

 Press under ½" (1.3 cm) at the lower edge; then press under 3" (7.5 cm) to form the hem. (The second fold should be even with the lower edge of the lining.) Pin the hem, placing pins perpendicular to the hem.

**Edgestitch (p. 51)** along the inner fold-line of the hem, **backstitching (p. 19)** at the beginning and end, and **removing the pins as you come to them (p. 45)**. Press the entire shade lightly.

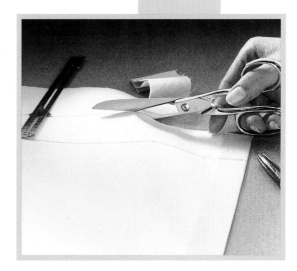

 On the lining side, draw a line across the top of the shade at the finished length. Draw a second line 1½" (3.8 cm) above it for the **mounting board projection.** Cut off excess fabric along the top line. Pin the layers together, and **FINISH** the upper edges together using a wide **ZIGZAG STITCH.**

*continued*

*continued*

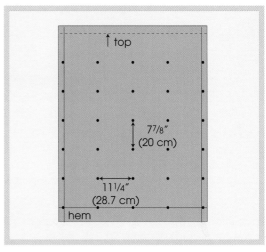

↑ top

7⅞" (20 cm)

11¼" (28.7 cm)

hem

**11** Diagram on graph paper the back side of the shade, indicating the finished length and width. Mark the hem 3" (7.5 cm) from the lower edge. Plan the **locations of rings** in columns spaced 8" to 12" apart (20.5 to 30.5 cm), with the outer columns ¾" (2 cm) from the outer edges of the shade. Space them in even horizontal rows 5" to 8" (12.5 to 20.5 cm) apart with the bottom row at the top of the hem and the top row on the marked line. Work through the following formula to determine ring locations. (We used these numbers for our shade on page 114; your numbers will probably be different.)

| | | |
|---:|:---:|:---|
| Finished width of shade: | | 45" (115 cm) |
| Divide by 12" (30.5 cm) | ÷ | 12" (30.5 cm) |
| and round up to the nearest whole number | = | 3¾" (9.5 cm) |
| to find the number of vertical spaces | | 4 |
| | | |
| Divide the finished width | | 45" (115 cm) |
| by the number of spaces | ÷ | 4 |
| to find distance between columns | = | 11¼" (28.7 cm) |
| | | |
| Length of shade from top of hem: | | 47" (120 cm) |
| Divide by 8" (20.5 cm) | ÷ | 8" (20.5 cm) |
| and round up to the nearest whole number | = | 5⅞" (14.7 cm) |
| to find the number of horizontal spaces | | 6 |
| | | |
| Divide the length | | 47" (120 cm) |
| by the number of spaces | ÷ | 6 |
| to find distance between horizontal rows | = | 7⅞" (20 cm) |

**12** Mark the locations for the rings on the lining side of the shade, according to your diagram. The bottom row of rings is at the upper edge of the hem; the top row is the determined distance below the top marked line. (There are no rings on the top line.) Pin horizontally through both layers of fabric at each mark.

**13** Thread a needle with a double strand of thread. Secure each ring with 4 or 5 small stitches, through both fabric layers. Reinforce all the rings in the bottom row with extra stitches because they carry the weight of the shade.

## Quick Reference

**Locations of rings.** A system of evenly spaced rings through which cords are run on the back of the shade make it possible to raise and lower the shade. When the rings are spaced in even columns and rows, the shade will fold neatly at regular intervals when raised.

**Hem pocket.** In forming the hem at the lower edge, 3" (7.5 cm) openings were left on the sides so that the hem is really a tube or "pocket" into which you will slide the weight bar.

**14** Insert the flat weight bar into the **hem pocket;** slipstitch (page 38) the openings closed along each side.

*continued*

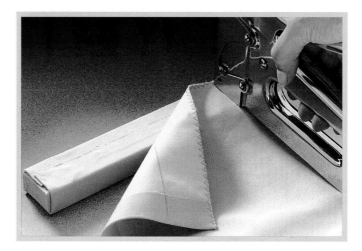

 **15** Remove the mounting board from the angle irons, if you are installing an outside mount. Staple the shade to the top of the mounting board, aligning the marked line to the top front edge of the board.

**16** Predrill the holes and insert screw eyes, centered, on the underside of the mounting board, aligning them to the columns of rings.

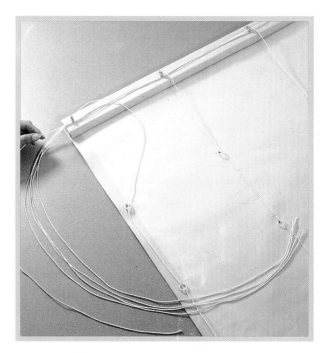

**17** On the side where you want the cords to hang, run cord through the first column of rings, through the top screw eye, and **at least halfway down the side.** Cut the cord and tie a non-slip knot at the bottom ring. Repeat for each column in order, running the cords also through the previous screw eyes. Apply glue to the knots for security.

Reattach the mounting board to the angle irons for an outside mount or install the mounting board directly to the underside of the window frame, inserting screws through predrilled holes, for an inside mount. Adjust the cords with the shade down so the tension on all cords is equal. Tie the cords in a knot just below the first screw eye. Braid the cords, insert them through a drapery pull, if desired, and knot and trim the ends.

*Quick Reference*

**At least halfway down the side.** Work on one column at a time, cutting the cord only after you have run the cord through the appropriate rings and screw eyes and determined the extra length needed for raising and lowering the shade. The extra length needed may depend on the location of the window and whether or not you want it to be accessible to children.

**Forming soft folds.** The first time you raise the shade, you may have to "train" it where to fold. As you raise the shade, pull the excess fabric between horizontal rows forward, forming gentle rolls. To help it "remember," leave the shade in the raised position for a day or two.

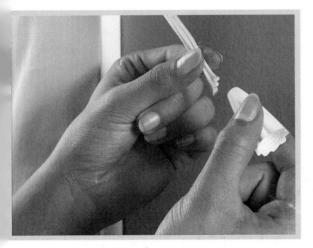

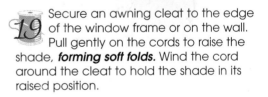 Secure an awning cleat to the edge of the window frame or on the wall. Pull gently on the cords to raise the shade, **forming soft folds.** Wind the cord around the cleat to hold the shade in its raised position.

*Congratulations!*

*With your own two hands, you have created a custom Roman shade that fits your window perfectly. You can't buy one ready-made from a store!*

# Glossary

**BACKSTITCH.** Several stitches are taken in the reverse direction at the beginning and end of a seam to keep the stitches from pulling out.

**BASTING.** Long, easy-to-remove stitches are sewn into the fabric temporarily, either by hand or by machine. Hand-basting stitches are used to hold layers of fabric and batting together for quilting. Machine-basting stitches are used to close a seam before inserting a zipper.

**BASTING TAPE.** Narrow tape that is sticky on both sides holds two pieces of fabric together so they will not shift while you are sewing.

**BIAS** refers to the diagonal direction of a piece of fabric. True bias is at a 45-degree angle to both the lengthwise and crosswise grains. Woven fabric has considerable stretch on the bias.

**CROSSWISE GRAIN.** On woven fabric, the crosswise grain runs perpendicular to the selvages. Fabric has slight "give" on the crosswise grain.

**CUT LENGTH** refers to the total length at which fabric should be cut for a project. It includes allowances for hems, seams, matching any prints, and, in the case of Roman shades, additional length for mounting.

**CUT WIDTH** refers to the total width at which fabric should be cut for a project. If more than one width of fabric is needed, the cut width refers to the entire panel after seams are sewn, including allowances for any side hems or seams.

**DIRECTIONAL PRINT.** The design printed on the fabric may have definite "up" and "down" directions, such as flowers growing upward. All pieces for a project should be cut so that the print will run in the correct direction when the project is finished.

**FABRIC IDENTIFICATION LABEL.** Found on every bolt or tube of fabric, this label informs you of the fiber content, width, and care method for the fabric. The labels on patterned decorator fabrics also indicate the length of the pattern repeat.

**FINISH.** To improve the durability of a seam, the raw edges are secured with a zigzag stitch that prevents them from fraying. This is important for items that must withstand repeated launderings. Finishing seams is especially recommended for items made with loosely woven fabric.

**FINISHED LENGTH** refers to the total length of a project after it is sewn. For a tablecloth, this includes twice the drop length; for a Roman shade finished length is measured from the top of the mounting board to the window sill or apron.

**FINISHED WIDTH** refers to the total width of a project after it is sewn. For a tablecloth, this includes twice the drop length. For an inside-mounted Roman shade, the finished width is the inside width of the window frame; for an outside-mounted shade, the finished width includes 1" (2.5 cm) beyond the frame on both sides.

**FLANGE** is a border of flat fabric that extends beyond the stitching line around the outer edge of a pillow, pillow sham, or duvet cover.

**GLUE-BASTE.** Secure two fabrics, or a fabric and a trim, together temporarily before sewing, using a fabric glue stick or dots of liquid fabric glue.

**GRAINLINES.** Woven fabrics have two grainlines, lengthwise and crosswise, which coincide with the yarns running in both directions, at right angles to each other. In order for a finished project to hang or lay straight, horizontal and vertical cuts must follow the grainlines exactly.

**HEM.** The outer edge of a project is given a neat finished appearance by turning under and securing the raw edge in one of several methods. It may be turned under twice and stitched, encasing the raw edge, as for the opening on a pillow sham. It may be turned under once and fused in place, as for the Roman shade. The round tablecloth is hemmed by stitching welting to the lower edge.

**INSIDE MOUNT** refers to a window treatment that is installed inside the window frame, usually flush with the front of the frame. In order to install an inside mount, the frame itself must be deep enough to accommodate the mounting board or rod without interfering with the operation of the window and allowing a clearance between the treatment and the glass.

**LENGTHWISE GRAIN.** On woven fabric, the lengthwise grain runs parallel to the selvages. Fabrics are generally stronger along the lengthwise grain.

**LINED TO THE EDGE** means that a fabric panel is backed with lining that is cut to the exact same size. The two pieces are joined together by a seam around the outer edge, with the raw edges of the seam allowances concealed between the layers.

**LINING** is a fabric backing sewn to the top fabric to provide extra body, protection from sunlight, and support for side hems or seams.

**MARK.** It is often necessary to give yourself temporary guidelines or guide points on the fabric for cutting, stitching, or matching seams. There are many tools and methods for doing this, such as marking pencils and pens, chalk dispensers, tape, or pins.

**MATCHING.** For a professional appearance when using decorator fabrics, stripes, plaids, and prints must line up across a seam from one fabric piece to another. In order to match pieces, they must be cut so the stripe or print falls in exactly the same place on both pieces.

**MITER.** Excess fabric on a corner is folded out at an angle to reduce bulk. This creates a smooth, neat appearance from both sides.

**NOMINAL LUMBER.** The actual measurement of nominal or "stock" lumber differs from the nominal size. A 1 × 2 board actually measures 3/4" × 1 1/2" (2 × 3.8 cm). Always measure boards for accuracy.

**OUTSIDE MOUNT** refers to a window treatment that is installed on the wall above the window frame and extends beyond the frame on the sides.

**PATTERN REPEAT,** a characteristic of decorator fabrics, is the lengthwise distance from one distinctive point in the pattern, such as the tip of a petal in a floral pattern, to the exact same point in the next pattern design.

**PIVOT.** Perfect corners are stitched by stopping with the needle down in the fabric at the exact corner before turning the fabric. To be sure the corner stitch locks, turn the handwheel until the needle goes all the way down and just begins to rise.

**PRESHRINKING.** Fabric that shrinks, especially natural-fiber fabric, shrinks most in the first laundering. If you intend to launder your finished project, wash and dry the fabric before cutting it out. Preshrink "dry-clean-only" fabrics by steaming them with your iron.

**PRESSING.** This step is extremely important to the success of your sewing projects. Select the heat setting appropriate for your fabric and use steam. Lift and lower the iron in an overlapping pattern. Do not slide the iron down the seam, as this can cause the fabric to stretch out of shape, especially on the crosswise grain or bias.

**PROJECTION** is the distance a mounting board or rod for a window treatment stands out from the wall.

**SEAM.** Two pieces of fabric are placed right sides together and joined near the edge with stitches. After stitching, the raw edges are hidden on the wrong side, leaving a clean, smooth line on the right side.

**SEAM ALLOWANCE.** Narrow excess fabric between the stitching line and the raw edge gives the seam strength and ensures that the stitches cannot be pulled off the raw edges.

**SELVAGE.** Characteristic of woven fabrics, these narrow, tightly woven outer edges should be cut away, or they may cause seams to pucker and may shrink excessively when washed.

**STRAIGHT STITCH.** Your machine forms stitch after stitch in a straight line because the needle does not change its position in this setting. You can alter the length of the stitch from long basting stitches to stitching in place. What you are really changing is the amount of fabric the feed dogs move with each stitch.

**ZIGZAG STITCH.** In this setting, the needle alternately moves from left to right with each stitch. You can alter the width of the needle swing as well as the length between stitches. A zigzag stitch that is twice as wide as it is long gives you a balanced stitch, appropriate for finishing seam allowances.

# Index

## A

Accessories, sewing
  machine, 10-11
Adjusting tension, 17
Allowance, seam, 125
  guide, 43

## B

Backstitch, 19, 124
Balancing tension, 16-17
Basting, 124
  machine, 81
  pin, 99
Basting tape, 26, 81, 124
Batting, 27
Beeswax, 21
Bent-handled dressmaker's
  shears, 23
Bias, 30, 124
Bias tape, single-fold, 26
  hemming method with, 47
Bobbins, 11
  winding, 13
Button and carpet
  thread, 28
Buttonhole length, 69
Buttons,
  for covering, 28
  sewing on, 39
Button-tufted cushion,
  105-111

## C

Carpenter's square, 22
Chair cushions, 105-112
Chalk, 22
Clipping seam allow-
  ances, 109
Cloth, press, 24
Corners, perfect, 61
Cover, duvet, 63-71
Covering buttons, 28
Crosswise grain, 30, 124
Cushions,
  button-tufted, 105-113
  ideas for, 112
Cut length, 124
Cutting boards, 25
Cutting fabrics, 34-35
Cutting foam, 107
Cutting tools, 23
Cut width, 124

## D

Decorator pillow, 75-83
  ideas for, 84-85
Decorator trims, flat, 29
Directional print, 124
Double-fold hems, 51
Dressmaker's shears,
  bent-handled, 23
Drop length, 43
Duvet covers, 63-73
  ideas for, 72

## E

Easing, 45
Edgestitch, 51
Embroidery presser foot, 11

## F

Fabric,
  cutting, 34-35
  marking, 22, 125
  matching patterns, 36-37
  preparing, 33
  preshrinking, 33, 125
  pressing, 24-25, 125
  shopping for, 32
  types of, 30
Fabric glue stick, 25, 51
Fabric identification
  label, 124
Fabric marking pens, 22
Finish, 124
Finished length, 124
Finished size, duvet cover, 65
Finished width, 124
Flange, 124
Flanged pillow shams, 55-61
Flat decorator trims, 29
Foam,
  cutting, 107
  polyurethane, 29
Fray preventer, liquid, 25
Fusible web, paper-
  backed, 26

## G

Gauge, hem, 22
General-purpose presser
  foot, 11

## Glossary, 124-125
Glue-baste, 124
Glues, 25
Glue stick, fabric, 51
Grain,
  crosswise, 30, 124
  lengthwise, 30, 125
  straight, 107
Grainlines, 124
Grosgrain ribbon, 29

## H

Hand-sewing supplies, 20-21
Hand stitches, 38-39
Hem, 124
  double-fold, 51
Hem gauge, 22
Hem pocket, 121
How to use this book, 6-7

## I

Inserting a sewing machine
  needle, 12
Inside mount, 115, 124
Irons, 24

## L

Length for buttonholes, 69
Lengthwise grain, 30, 125
Lined table runner, 86-93
Lined to the edge, 125
Lining, 125
Liquid fray preventer, 25
Lumber, nominal, 25

## M

Machine basting, 81
Marking fabric, 22, 125
Marking tools, 22
Matching patterns,
  36-37, 125
Measuring tools, 22
Mitering, 125
Mounting board, 115-117
  projection, 119, 125

## N

Napkins, super easy, 101
Needles,
  hand-sewing, 38
  sewing machine, 10, 12

Needle threader, 21
Nominal lumber, 125

O

Outside mount, 115, 125

P

Paper-backed fusible
  web, 26
Parts of a sewing
  machine, 9
Pattern repeat, 32, 125
Patterns, fabric, matching,
  36-37
Pencils, chalk and
  graphite, 22
Pens, fabric marking, 22
Perfect corners, 61
Pillows,
  decorator, 75-83
  forms, 29
  ideas for, 84-85
  shams, flanged, 55-61
Pin-basting, 99
Pincushion, 21
Pins, 20
Pivot, 125
Placemats, quilted, 95-100
  ideas for, 102-103
Point turner, 25
Polyurethane foam, 29
Preparing fabric, 33
Preshrinking fabric, 33, 125
Press cloth, 24
Presser feet, 11
Pressing, 47, 125
  tools, 24-25
Printed on-grain, 35
Projection, 125
  mounting board, 119

Q

Quilted placemats, 95-100
  ideas for, 102-103
Quilting lines, 97

R

Rectangular tablecloth,
  49-51
Ribbon, grosgrain, 29
Rings, locations of, 121
Ripper, seam, 23, 81
Roman shades, 115-123

Round tablecloth, 41-47
Ruler, transparent, 22
Runners, table,
  ideas for, 102-103
  lined, 86-93

S

Scissors, 23
Seam allowance, 125
  guide, 43
Seam ripper, 23, 81
Seam roll, 25
Seams, 125
  sewing, 18-19
Selvages, 30, 125
Sewing machine, 8
  accessories, 10-11
  adjusting tension, 17
  balancing tension, 16-17
  basting on, 81
  inserting the needle, 12
  needles, 10
  parts, 9
  testing tension, 16
  threading, 14-15
  winding the bobbin, 13
Sew-through buttons,
  sewing on, 39
Shades, Roman, 115-123
Shams, pillow,
  flanged, 55-61
  ideas for, 72
Shank buttons, sewing
  on, 39
Shears, dressmaker's,
  bent-handled, 23
Single-fold bias tape, 26
Slipstitching, 38
Sole plate, Teflon-coated, 24
Special products, 26-29
Special-purpose presser
  foot, 11
Stitches,
  backstitch, 19, 124
  basting, 81, 124
  edgestitch, 51
  hand, 38-39
  slip, 38
  straight, 125
  zigzag, 125
Supplies, sewing, 20-25
  cutting tools, 23
  hand-sewing, 20-21
  measuring and marking
    tools, 22
  pins, 20

pressing tools, 24-25
Symmetry, 107

T

Tablecloths,
  ideas for, 52-53
  rectangular, 49-51
  round, 41-47
Table runners,
  ideas for, 102-103
  lined, 86-93
Tape,
  basting, 26, 81, 124
  bias, single-fold, 26
  twill, 27
Tape measure, 22
Tension, balancing, 16-17
Thimble, 21
Thread, button and
  carpet, 28
Threading needles,
  for hand sewing, 38
  for machine sewing, 14-15
Thread jams, 19
Tools,
  cutting, 23
  measuring and
    marking, 22
  pressing, 24-25
Transparent ruler, 22
Trims, flat decorator, 29
Twill tape, 27

W

Walking presser foot, 11
Web, fusible, paper-
  backed, 26
Welted hem on round
  tablecloth, 41-47
Welting, 27
Winding bobbins, 13
Window shades, Roman,
  115-123

Y

Yardstick, 22

Z

Zigzag stitch, 125
Zipper presser foot, 11
Zippers, 28
  on pillows, 80-83
Zipper stops, 81